पेगासी

A COLLECTION OF POEMS

खुशी धीमान

To those who find poetry in mundane moments

क्रम-सूची

क्रम-सूची

पावती (स्वीकृति)

(ACKNOWLEDGEMENTS)

As they say- "A heart full of gratitude is a magnet for miracles", and I am, indeed, extremely grateful to some people in my life. Without these people, I would not have been able to discover my potential.

First and foremost, I want to thank my parents, who never discouraged me from writing, and who have always been a pillar of support for me in every way. They have encouarged me to make my decisions for myself, whether it be what to wear or the matter of my career. Thanks to them for making me see my wings, and teaching me how to fly.

I also want to thank my teachers, who guided me to use my potential, and made me see things about myself that I was unaware of. Thankyou, for motivating me, giving me opportunities to explore my caliber, and shaping me into a strong, new vessel. Special thanks to Mona ma'am and Gurleen ma'am, my former Hindi and English teachers respectively, who are a mentor to me. Thanks to Raminder ma'am, who always believes in me.

Next, I want to thank my friends. They praise me on my acheivements, criticize me when necessary, and, most importantly, motivate me when I am low on self-confidence. Thanks to my best friend, Marianne, who is my favourite person in the world and an inseparable part of my being. Thankyou for tolerating my endless nonsense and letting me tolerate yours, and for being there for me, always. Big thanks to Pratima, author of 'Cortney: The Game of Destiny' and 'Cortney: The Change in Destiny', whose talent and boldness is ever inspiring to me. Thankyou Jhanvi, a special friend of mine who very kindly consented to write the foreword for this book.

And a big thanks to Shereen, publishing consultant at Notion Press, who helped me out at several stages of the process. She was always there and quick to respond with a solution to any problem I faced.

Credit where it is due- thanks to the makers of Google Deep Dream Generator, because that is what I used to design the cover of my book. (And I love how it turned out!)

Thanks to Wylan, who is very dear to me for a number of reasons, and thankyou ma'am Leigh Bardugo for creating him and writing the Six of Crows duology. I am so very grateful to Jack Wolfe for changing my life for the better, and no amount of thanks is enough in this regard.

Thank you, my readers, for taking the time to read these fragments of my thoughts and imagination.

Above all, my heartfelt gratitude to my Gods, who never let the smile fade from my face for long, and whose footprints I can see beside mine at every step.

प्रस्तावना

(FOREWORD)

By Jhanvi Pendyala

Okay, so I'm a person who doesn't know how forewords go, and this is my first time actually writing one, and for this opportunity I want to thank my sakhi. Starting off, I want to tell you about Khushi. I haven't met her in real life (yet), but from what I've experienced, she is a Wylan van Sunshine- cute and dangerous at the same time. She is the living embodiment of "kill them with kindness".

Khushi is true to her name, she brings happiness wherever she is around and to whomever she is talking. She's beautiful inside out, trustworthy, kind hearted, talented and all in all, a WONDERFUL person we honestly don't deserve. She will always help you if you ask for it and if she knows she can.

Talking about her writing skills, her poetry and words are indeed very powerful. Her Hindi and English poetries are equally moving and simply yet wonderfully thought-provoking. I know there are some people out here who might be a little skeptical whether to start this book or not (because you might not be into poetry or for some other reason) but let me tell you, these poems are relatable, heartwarming and tear-jerking, and definitely a must read!

    - Jhanvi Pendyala, a fellow poet and writer

Can I Have Your Attention Please?

Other books by the author: 1) काव्यांजलि

2) Buried Emotions: Only the Soul can Reveal (co-author, editor and compiler)

3) Lily (poem published in the anthology)

Available on: www.poetryworld.org (काव्यांजलि and Buried Emotions)

www.thewriteorder.com (Lily)

भूमिका

(PREFACE)

Dear readers,

Where do I start? What a peculiar thing, isn't it, that we often miss the things going on around us because we are so busy imagining conversations or things that we want to talk about, but forget all about it when the moment comes? It happens more frequently and more often than I'd like to admit. But I hope you will pardon my forgetfulness for now.

There is a famous quote by John Green that holds true for me: "My thoughts are stars I cannot fathom into constellations." My thoughts occur in the form of unconnected chunks, and poetry is the thread through which I weave them, making a pearl necklace out of them.

I read poetry much less than I would like to, and mostly read novels. However, I have a home in it, in poetry. It comes much more naturally to me than prose. Even people who are not much interested in literature find solace in it from time to time. As I like to say- profession sustains livelihood, passion sustains life. So please, for your sake, visit your passions every once in a while. Read the book you have been meaning to, re-watch your comfort movie, go out for a walk, sleep an extra hour today, sing in the shower, dance to silly songs till you run out of breath, because we often neglect these joy-bringing things, and while the surface seems to be put-together, the inside slips away, where it cannot be retreived. You may forget what you wanted to say, like me, but never forget to give your brains the happy chemical!

That being said, I want to introduce you to how this book came into being. Now, I would love to tell you that I worked day and night to reach here, that this book is a product of my sweat and blood, that I overcame every obstacle my way to accomplish this; but that is simply not the case. There is no special story behind this book. It is merely a compilation of the poems I have written over the years. I did not sweat for it.

Actually, scratch that. I did sweat a lot, in finding all my poems. They were scattered all over random pages, the margins of my very old rough notebooks, my chats with my friends, and here and there. That part was a lot of hardwork, finding all those poems. And the typing and proof-reading was not very easy either. But apart from that, there was no such difficulty or "struggle" as such in the process, and we should discard the notion that all good things come through struggle. (Thankyou, Notion Press, for making the publishing process a piece of cake!) The point is, art exists for freedom and relaxation. If we make struggle a part of art, that snatches away the very purpose of it. Instead, we should learn to enjoy it and make it enjoyable for others. So I genuinely hope these not-very-significant thoughts of mine can leave some impact, however small it may be.

One's deeds are the path to her soul, but her words are the lamplights along the way, without which you would be lost in the dark forever. Hence, reading someone's words is a strangely intimate thing. These words- my words- show you the path to my soul. I hope you like it there.

(Please bring a flashlight, just in case it gets dark!)

1. 17 Years

Are 17 years
Really that long,
Mother?
Then why do I feel so young?
Are 17 years
Really that brief,
Grandmother?
Then why do I feel so old?
Why do I still fear ghosts,
But not play with my dolls anymore?
Why are there pieces of past in me,
Ill-fitting with today?
Is youth a tornado,
Grandfather?
Scattering and changing
Everything I knew
And shaping me into someone new,
Leaving behind remnants
Stained with love?

2. Childhood- A Place

A few nights ago
My cousins and I,
Late after bedtime had crawled by,
Stayed wide awake,
As you do when you are young
And delight is constant,
My mother and aunt telling us to go to sleep.
After some time, we tired,
And shut our eyes dutifully,
Pursed our lips,
Waiting for the dreams to come.
A handful of breaths later,
My little cousin,
Whom we thought asleep,
Burst into laughter, for no apparent reason!
And so did I, followed by my brother,
And the other cousin.
There, in the silence of the dark,
Rang the bells of our laughter,
Scaring away the Devil,
While the elders looked at us reproachfully,
Astonished, as to what had gotten into us!
But,

In that moment, I realised
That childhood isn't a time period.
No, childhood is a place.
A place, where laughs are contagious,
Where time never ticks,
Where anger never stays long,
A place where grass is always green
And red and blue and purple and pink,
And any colour you can imagine,
A place full of smiles passed without hesitation,
A place indifferent to differences,
Where the hearth always stays warm,
Where masks don't exist,
A place of innocent barters,
Where no love remains hidden.
I realised all this in that moment,
And in that one moment,
Aeons could have been dwarfed.

3. Love And Hate

Sometimes.
Sometimes, I really hate the people I love.
I hate them,
Despise them,
In a way you can only despise your loved ones.
I want to get away from them,
But again,
Who else will I go to?
Perhaps hate, after all,
Is not the opposite of love.
Rather,
It is the curse
That comes with every boon,
The thorns on a rose,
The backside of a beautiful tapestry.

4. Whispers In The Woods

Do not turn if you hear
Whispers in the woods.
Do not reply,
For they will follow you.
Do not call for anyone,
You never know
Who is waiting to answer.
Do not stare if you see
Glowing eyes in the woods,
Or they might come alive.
Do not stay too long in the woods,
For they will consume you,
And you will become the woods.

5. Anger And Grief

Anger and grief,
Anger and grief,
Which is worse-
Anger or grief?
Anger hollows out
A cavity in you,
And grief fills that cavity
With heavy cement-
Until everything seems heavy,
Even your eyelids seem too heavy to lift-
Desperately attempting to hold everything
together,
Anger rules over tongue,
Grief hides in chest.
Anger seeks to hurt,
Grief is because of hurt.
Anger or grief,
Which is worse?
That, a creature silly as me does not know.
What she knows is that
Worse is a child
Born out of the two.
A child of anger and grief.

Such a child is rough,
All sharp edges and heavy glances.
It yearns to be seen
And, at the same time,
Hides in the lap of shadows.
Anger and grief,
Anger and grief-
They devour it from inside,
Till there is nothing left but
Echoes,
Echoes,
Echoes.

6. In The Gardens Of Heaven

Tender hands touch
The necklace of clouds
And the pearls scatter to earth.
I pick one up
And swallow it.
Wings grow out of my back then
And I float above my head-
I am huma no more.
An existence, an energy,
A concept-
Is all I am.

7. All I Am

Is all I am
A memory?
Etched
In someone's head;
Unopened, untouched,
Waiting to be read?

Is all I am
A memory?
Real
But really not;
Alone, cold,
With barely a thought?

Is all I am
A memory?
Forgotten,
Covered in dust;
Learning, teaching,
Never ever to trust?

Is all I am
A memory?

Hidden,
But occassionally peeping;
Thinking, thinking,
Am I worth keeping?

8. Broken Glass

Who would love me?
For who loves broken glass?
Broken glass,
Cracked glass,
Fragile glass.
Glass that could shatter
Upon a touch?
For who sees the battle
That made it crack?
The fall,
The hit,
The load?
A ragpicker, however,
Picks it up tenderly
And values each piece.
He caresses the cracked pieces.
The cracked,
The jagged,
The broken pieces,
Pieces that make his fingers bleed,
Pieces that very well
Echo his soul.

9. Irony Of Colours

Violet grapes, sweet and sour,
Indigo sky at midnight,
Blue ocean, majestic and calm,
Green earth, fertile and motherly,
Yellow and pink flowers,
Orange dawns, peaceful as home,
Red pomegranates, the colour of blood-
We love,
We cherish,
We protect.
Fair skin,
Brown skin,
Dark skin-
We hate,
We discriminate,
We kill.

10. Rain And Faith

I begin to question my faith,
Suddenly it rains,
And,
Just like that,
I am a believer again.

11. The Grass Will Sing Our Song

No one but the grass
Will sing our song.

It will remember
How we lay on it,
The moon glowing above us,
Jealous that you were mine.

It will remember
That eah evening we came,
We came and became
What we were,
Losing what we were not
In the blades of grass.

It will remember
The wild choir of hatred
Swirling around us,
Like a cyclone around the Eye.

It will remember
How the blade was thrust into your body,

Once, twice, then thrice,
And then into mine,
My blood becoming ichor
At the touch of yours.

It will remember
How we lay there again,
For one last, eternal time,
Our final breaths mingling.

It will remember, and,
In the aeons to come,
No one but the grass will sing our song.
And till the final dusk of the universe,
We will listen to the rasping,
Acheing song of ours,
My love.

12. You

When I close my eyes,
Everything dies,
And God is born anew,
But the only thing that remains,
My Love,
Is you,
You,
You.

13. Colours and Curses

Colours shimmer
At the periphery of my vision
But when I look
There are none-
A mirage in this desert.
It was not always a desert,
Nor the colours a mirage.
Trees grew here, and flowers bloomed,
Squirrels chased each other,
Winds danced,
And streams played with the clouds.
Of course, all this is nothing now-
A story, a memory,
For a mother's curse can upturn God,
What is a mortal life then-
A life already full of curses?

14. 'Eternal' Glory

Into the forest I go,
Where the trees tell me a story,
Of their own
Fallen, 'eternal' glory.

15. For Ever

I used to rest in your arms,
And now on your grave,
I shall sleep forever.

You, lifeless and I,
Existing without life,
Dust and bones only
For unrequired company.

You don't breathe,
And I don't want to.
I dare not inhale your absence,
Fearing that it might wipe away
From my mind
The treasure of your memory.

Your name and face
Are a blissful memory
Keeping me sane
While slowly and lovingly consuming me,
Quite unlike the way they consumed you
For loving me.

Realisation strikes me,
And I get jealous of the earth,
For she is embracing you,
And I am not.

My scream pierces the stillness of death-
The angels of grief have found me.
The dead cover their ears,
They dare not hear the mourning of a lover,
Or they might die again.

With every ounce of hope
And energy left in me,
I call your name,
Beg you to come,
To come and take me with you.

And there you are, at last!
You head in my direction,
Your face beautiful and pale
As the moon herself.
You come to where my body lies.
Ah, how temporary it is!
How fragile, how mortal.
You wipe the blood away,
And turn towards me now.
Taking my hand in yours,

Embracing me.
At last, we are now together,
For ever.

16. Violet Love

Lightning strikes the sky
Same shade of bright violet
As love.
I watch from afar
As fascinated as afraid.
The thing that could destroy anyone,
The thing that lights everything up,
The thing that makes night into day-
I knew it would consume me.
But what could be more beautiful
Than to be consumed
With love
By love?

17. Humanity- A Phoenix

Often, I think,
That humanity is dead.
But, just like a phoenix,
It rises from the ashes,
Stronger than ever.

18. I Become The Trees

Into the forest I go,
Where the trees sing for me,
And the birds say hello.

I stand and gaze
At the trunks of Pine-
A forever running maze.

I sit down in the leaves
That once danced on the Pine,
Now silenced forever
By the ghost of time.

The moon peeks at me
Through the broken heart
Of a mourning tree.

And there I sleep,
Caressed by the cool night's breeze,
And there I become-
I become the trees.

19. Mysteries

In the crinkly yellow pages of a diary,
In the lost words of a lover's shayari;
In the twinkle of the stars,
In the lonely, empty cars-
Mysteries, mysteries, mysteries.

In the voices in the woods,
In the old, forgotten routes;
In warm, lovingly knitted sweaters,
In stormy, rainy weathers-
Mysteries, mysteries, mysteries.

In the crawing of the crow,
In the scarlet on the snow;
In the sunset, in the sunrise,
In the irises of your eyes-
Mysteries, mysteries, mysteries.

20. Maa's Love

My Maa's love cannot be measured,
It is not a quantity,
It is the foundation
Of my identity.

My Maa's love cannot be judged,h
It is not a law case,
It is just like
A warm, lovely embrace.

My Maa's love cannot be calculated,
It is not like maths,
It has a srange beauty
Even in its wrath.

My Maa's love cannot be bought,
It is not a grocery,
Its magic is greater,
Than any other sorcery.

Yes, my Maa's love can be valued,
It is the purest emotion,
Heals every wound-

It is such a divine potion!

21. Love Letter

The sweetest of dreams,
The prettiest of the skies,
Bestowed this gift,
Upon I.
If there is such a thing as home,
It is in your eyes.

You walk, walk, walk,
Where the moon shines,
And I embrace insanity
In your shrines,
Forgetting the line
Between blood and wine.

I love alike
The gentle breeze of your laughter,
And the tornado of your rage.
Beyond you,
The earth is a cage.
Come, take me away,
I am dying of craze.

Why do people look down upon craze?

It is sweet, It is lovely,
It has you in it.
And I wouldn't mind,
If the cost of seeing you
Includes my breaths.

But oh, where there is love,
There is tragedy.
You know not of my heart,
Know not of me.
Thus, o shooting star!
Take my love letter to thy goddess,
And tell her that I
Will wait for her
Till oblivion.

22. The Way You Look Tonight

The way you look tonight,
Stars suddenly seem less bright.

A mist settles in.
It approaches you slowly,
And smiles.
You open your mouth to talk,
But I hear music,
Ah, the divine music!
In that moment I see
A goddess in you.

Your dress flutters
In the windy autumn night,
And the stars suddenly seem less bright.

The darkness blushes
And strokes your cheek.
You laugh a muted laugh,
Hold up your umbrella,
And tread silently
On the worn grey pavement.

In that moment I see
A victorian lady in you.

As I watch you
In the lonely, lonely night,
The stars suddenly seem less bright.

The road of fate twists and oh,
You stand in front of me.
Your honey eyes dance,
Reflecting your train of thoughts.
And in that moment, in you,
I see the real you.

A newspaper comes flying at me.
It reads-
"Isabella Jane found dead."
As I look at your picture
Under the article, in the yellow lamplight,
The stars suddenly seem less bright.

23. When You Are Afraid

When you are afraid to ask,
Don't keep quiet.
When you are afraid to stand up,
Don't fall back down.
When you are afraid to face something,
Don't turn your back.
When you are afraid to speak up,
Don't fall silent.
When you are afraid to continue,
Don't stop.
And, most importantly,
When you are afraid to love,
Don't spread hate.

24. यह जीवन है

यह जीवन है।
यहां खूंखार जीव बड़े हैं,
अटल वृक्ष मार्ग रोक खड़े हैं।
ऐसी कठिनाइयों से भरा वन है,
यह जीवन है।
इसके दस मुख दुराचारी,
शक्तिशाली, अत्यंत अहंकारी।
ऐसा दशग्रीव रावण है,
यह जीवन है।
माया है यह क्षणभंगुर,
पनपते जिसमें मोह के अंकुर।
एक क्षण अडिग, और लुप्त अगले क्षण है,
यह जीवन है।

25. इंद्रधनुष

कैसे बनता है इंद्रधनुष?
देखता है ईश्वर
कि कैसे उसके बनाए रंग
अदृश्य-से हो गए हैं,
और चारों दिशाओं में दिखाई देते हैं केवल
घृणा और लोभ के रंग।
यह दृश्य देखकर रो देता है वह,
और इन्ही अश्रुओं को
जब सूर्य समेटता है
तो बिखर जाते हैं सात मोतियों में-
संसार को पुनः रंगने का
एक अनंत प्रयास।

26. नारायणी सेना

यहाँ सब चाहें नारायणी सेना,
श्री कृष्ण की है अब चाह किसे?
कर्म-हीन यहाँ बैठे सब हैं,
धर्म की दिखाएं राह किसे?

27. यह सागर अब मंथ डाल

तूफानों से यारी कर,
आलस्य का संहारी बन।
आज निज सामर्थ्य की
समस्त सीमाएं लाँघ,
यह सागर अब मंथ डाल।
लहरों से मात खाकर ही
रत्न हाथ लग पाता है,
हर गोता उस गोताखोर का
व्यर्थ नहीं जाता है।
पा ले अपने रत्न, अपने स्वप्न को,
तोड़ मछुआरों के जाल,
यह सागर अब मंथ डाल।
लहरों के दर्पण में
स्वयं से स्वयं को मिला,
आज़ादी का अमृत खोज,
बेड़ियों को विष पिला।
हृदय को जगा, रक्त में ला उबाल,
यह सागर अब मंथ डाल।
हर हारी कोशिश से
अपना हौंसला सजा,
कांप जाए अंबर भी
ऐसा रुदन मचा।

चूर हो जाए हर नौका,
तू कर पुनः निर्माण,
यह सागर अब मंथ डाल।

28. आसमां की शिकस्त

आसमां भी उनसे शिकस्त पाया करता है,
कि इंद्रधनुष उनकी ज़ुल्फो में उतर आया करता है।
आईने को जो होता है दीदार उनका,
तो आइना भी संवर जाए करता है।

29. कलम की जय बोल

आज कलम की जय बोल!
दिए जिसने ज्ञान के
सात समंदर खोल,
आज कलम की जय बोल।
जिसके कारण आज प्रत्यक्ष हैं
इतिहास, विज्ञान, भूगोल,
आज कलम की जय बोल।
जिसकी रेखा मात्र से
मनुष्य का भाग्य गया डोल,
आज कलम की जय बोल।
इसका मूल्य नहीं है,
ये तो है अनमोल,
आज कलम की जय बोल।

30. प्रकृति का यौवन

एक पहाड़ ने दूसरे को पैगाम भिजवाया है,
बहती पवन का मधुर संगीत सुनाया है।
पक्षियों ने कोलाहल सा मचाया है,
चंद्रमा ने अपना कोमल मुखड़ा दिखाया है।
अलकनंदा के हृदय में उफान उतर आया है,
वृक्षों ने विद्रोह का मन बनाया है।
बादलों का चंचल रूप सामने आया है,
तारों संग आंख-मिचौली का खेल रचाया है।
यूं ही नहीं वसंत ने
प्रकृति को उसका यौवन लौटाया है!

31. भारत- एक कविता

भारत एक कविता है!
सुर व लय में पिरोया गया मोती,
मधुर संगीत की ध्वनि,
सौंदर्य की मिसाल!
अलंकार से भरपूर,
सादगी से सुसज्जित,
इसके शब्दों के मायने
सबके लिए भिन्न!
कर्णप्रिय, चक्षुप्रिय, हृदयप्रिय-
भारत एक कविता है!

32. हे ईश्वर

हे ईश्वर! तुम ही मेरे रक्षक हो,
तुम हो मेरे गुरु।
तुमने ही तो की थी मेरे
श्वासों की यात्रा शुरू।
हे ईश्वर! तुम ही मेरे मार्गदर्शक हो,
तुम हो मेरा सहारा।
तुमने ही तो बदली मेरे
विचार-विमर्शों की धारा।
हे ईश्वर! तुम ही मेरे बंधु हो,
तुम हो मेरे सखा।
तुमने ही तो शीश पर मेरे
अपना हाथ रखा।
हे ईश्वर! तुम ही परमेश्वर हो,
तुम ही मेरे मित्र।
फिर भी, हे ईश्वर!
तुम हो बहुत विचित्र।

33. भूमि जज़्बातों की

मेरे दिल की धड़कन धक-धक-धक नहीं,
जण-गण-मन ही गाती है,
किसी अन्य का नाम नहीं,
बस वंदे मातरम् सुनाती है।
रूह में भी मेरी
बसते हैं वही तीन रंग पवित्र,
हृदय में भी छपा है
भारत माँ का ही चित्र।
केसरिया, श्वेत और हरा-
यही मेरा श्रृंगार है,
जय हिंद, जय भारत-
यही मेरा सत्श्रीअकाल, अदब और नमस्कार है।
भारत मेरी भूमि है,
और क्या बात करूँ सौगातों की,
भारत केवल देश नहीं,
भूमि है जज़्बातों की,
भूमि है जज़्बातों की।

34. इश्क़ का रंग

इश्क़ का कोई रंग नहीं,
और हर रंग भी इश्क़ का है।
इश्क़ धरती-सा सहनशील है,
इसलिए भूरा है।
इश्क़ सूरज जैसा तेजस्वी है,
इसलिए लाल है।
इश्क़ चांद-सा शीतल,
तो श्वेत भी।
इश्क़ प्रकृति-सा निस्वार्थ है,
तो हरा भी है।
गुलाब सा है यह-
खुशबू भी है, और कांटे भी,
इसलिए गुलाबी रंग है इसका।
विष के समान घातक है, तो नीला भी है।
इश्क़ पूजा है, तो पीला भी है।
किसी के लिए कलंक, तो किसी के लिए काजल-
इसलिए काला भी है।
इंद्रधनुष को पानी में घोल कर पी गया था ऊपरवाला एक
दिन,
जब आंसू निकले, तो इश्क़ बन गया!

35. सौगंध खाकर कहती हूँ

तेरा छुआ तो विष भी अमृत हो जाए,
तेरे स्पर्श मात्र से ही
उजाड़ भी समृद्ध हो जाए|
तू अपने सागर नेत्रों से देखे जो एक बार,
सौगंध खाकर कहती हूँ-
रावण भी राम में परिवर्तित हो जाए!
जहाँ पाँव तू रख दे
वह माटी पावन हो जाए,
तू एक बार आ तो सही प्यारे,
और देख कैसे अकाल में सावन हो जाए!
तेरे साथ तो हार भी जीत हो जाए,
तेरे मुख से निकलने वाला
शब्द-शब्द गीत हो जाए|
तू अपने साक्षात् दर्शन दे उसे जो एक बार,
सौगंध खाकर कहती हूँ-
घृणा को भी तुझसे प्रीत हो जाए!
तेरे आने की देर है,
घमासान युद्ध क्रीड़ा हो जाए,
तू एक बार मुस्कुरा तो सही प्यारे,
और देख कैसे गायब सारी पीड़ा हो जाए!
तेरी दृष्टि-भर से अहित भी हित हो जाए,
तेरे कहने मात्र से सारे
रंग आसमानी एकत्रित हो जाएँ|

तू मरते हुए को संबोधित करे जो एक बार,
सौगंध खाकर कहती हूँ-
सद्गति प्राप्त उसे मोक्ष सहित हो जाए!
तेरे पाँव को छूने वाला
हर कंकर हीरा हो जाए,
तेरे पढ़ने से यह कविता भक्ति रस,
और देख कैसे यह कवयित्री मीरा हो जाए,
यह कवयित्री मीरा हो जाए!

www.ingramcontent.com/pod-product-compliance
Lightning Source LLC
Chambersburg PA
CBHW022109150726
47990CB00003B/1299